# alone
# together

## clayton junior

### words & pictures

high

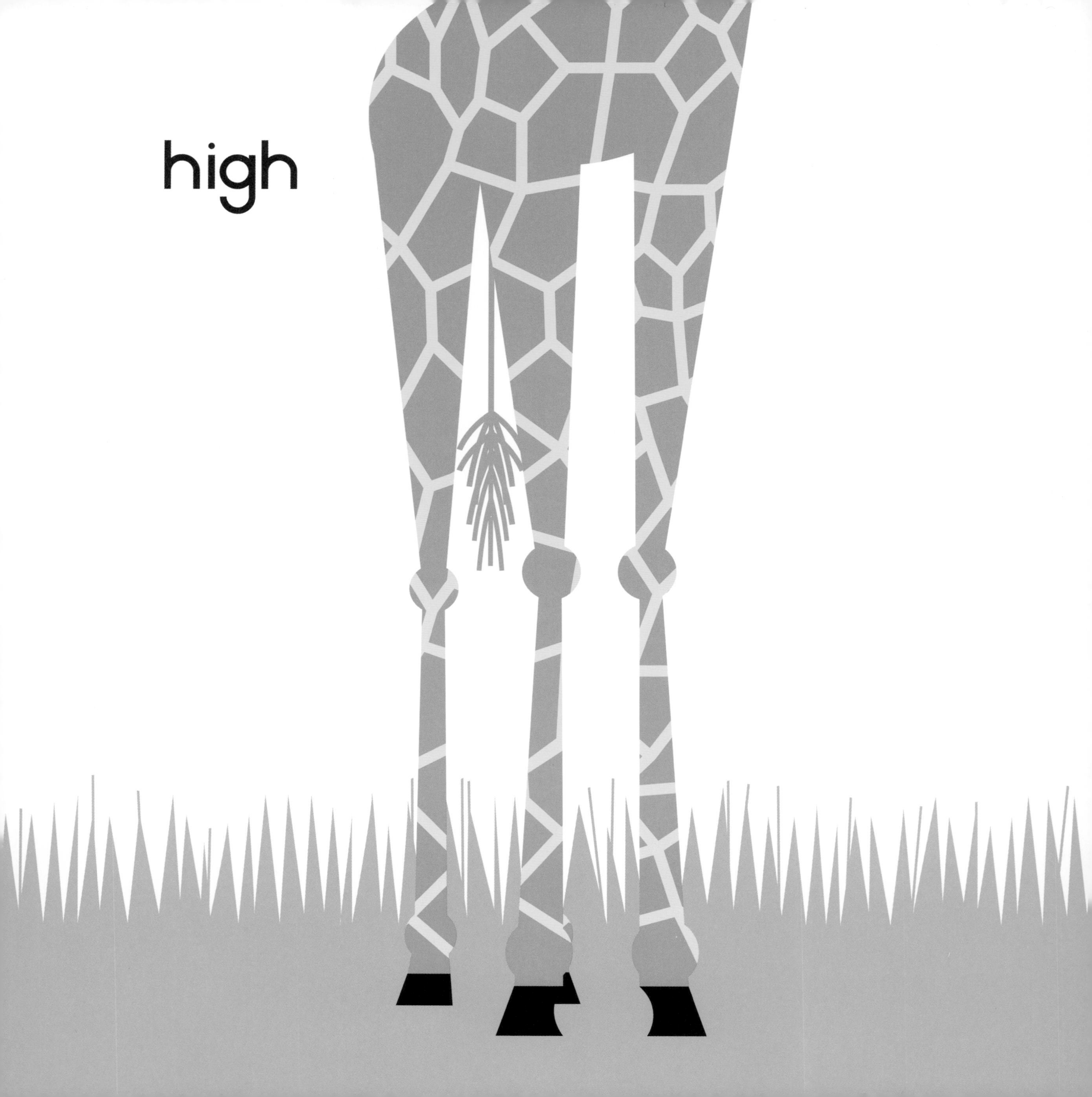

**The item should be returned or renewed by the last date stamped below.**

Dylid dychwelyd neu adnewyddu'r eitem erbyn y dyddiad olaf sydd wedi'i stampio isod.

PILLGWENLLY

25 JUL 2018

To renew visit / Adnewyddwch ar
**www.newport.gov.uk/libraries**

This paperback edition first published in 2017
First published in hardback in 2016 by
words & pictures, Part of The of Quarto Group,
The Old Brewery, 6 Blundell Street, London N7 9BH

British Library Cataloguing in Publication Data
available on request

ISBN: 978-1-91027-754-6

1 3 5 7 9 8 6 4 2

Printed in China

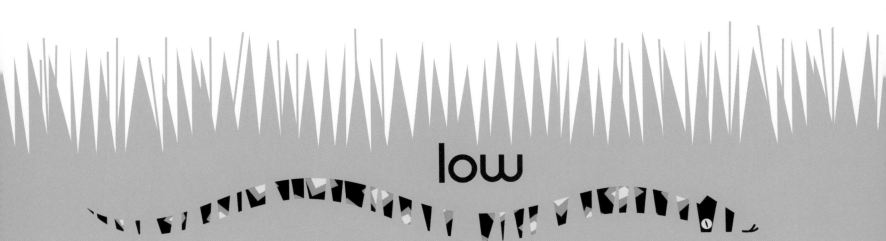

messy

LOUD

quiet

moving

still

far

close

fancy

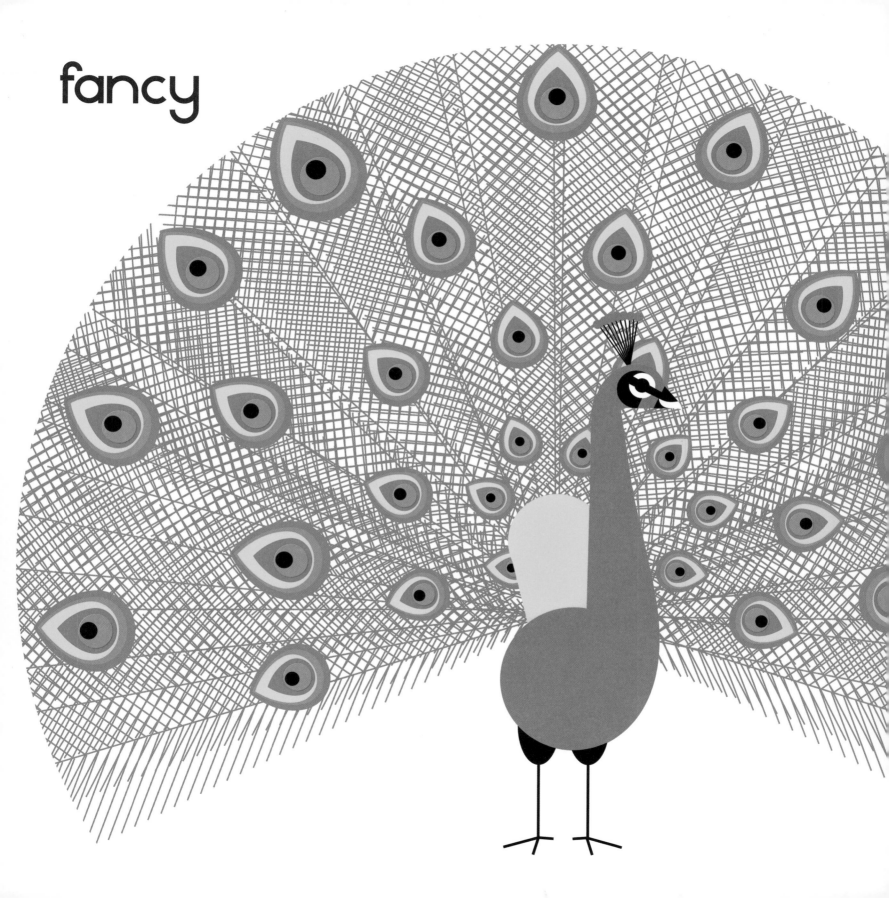

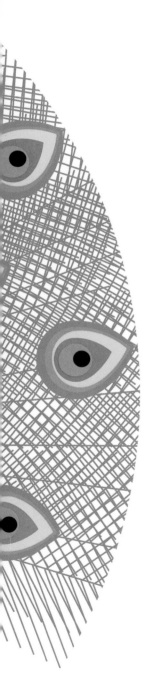

sober

slow

fast

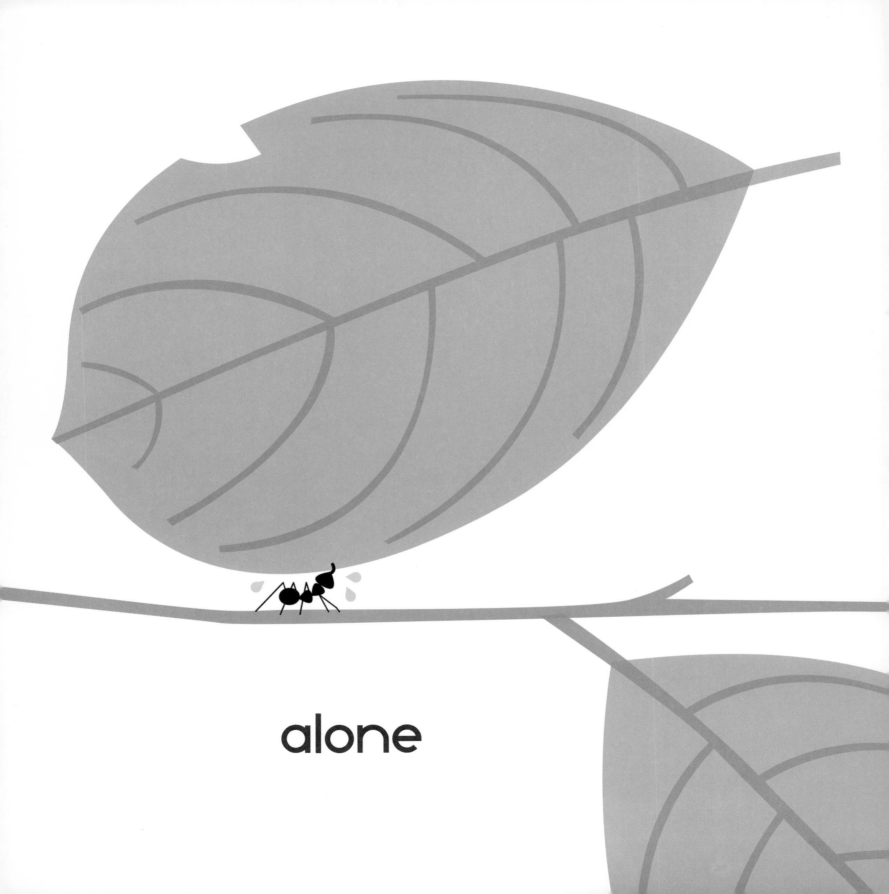

alone

together

sturdy

fragile

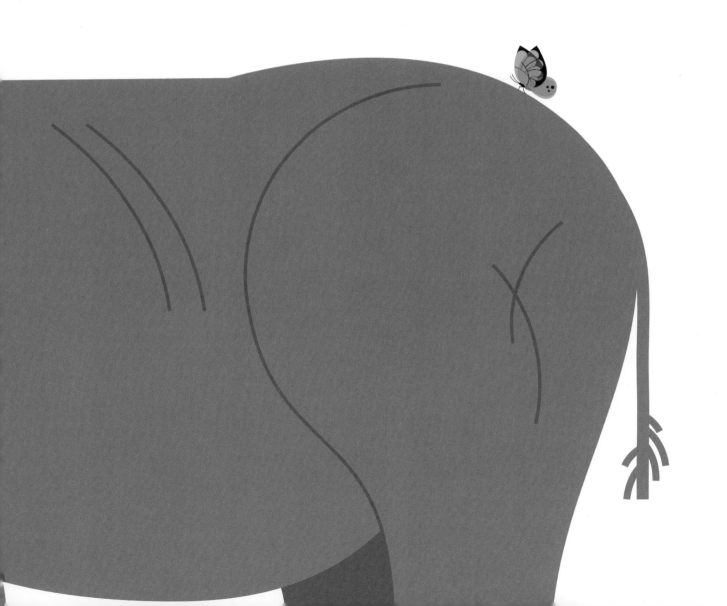

stripes

spots

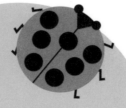

# spiky

soft

big

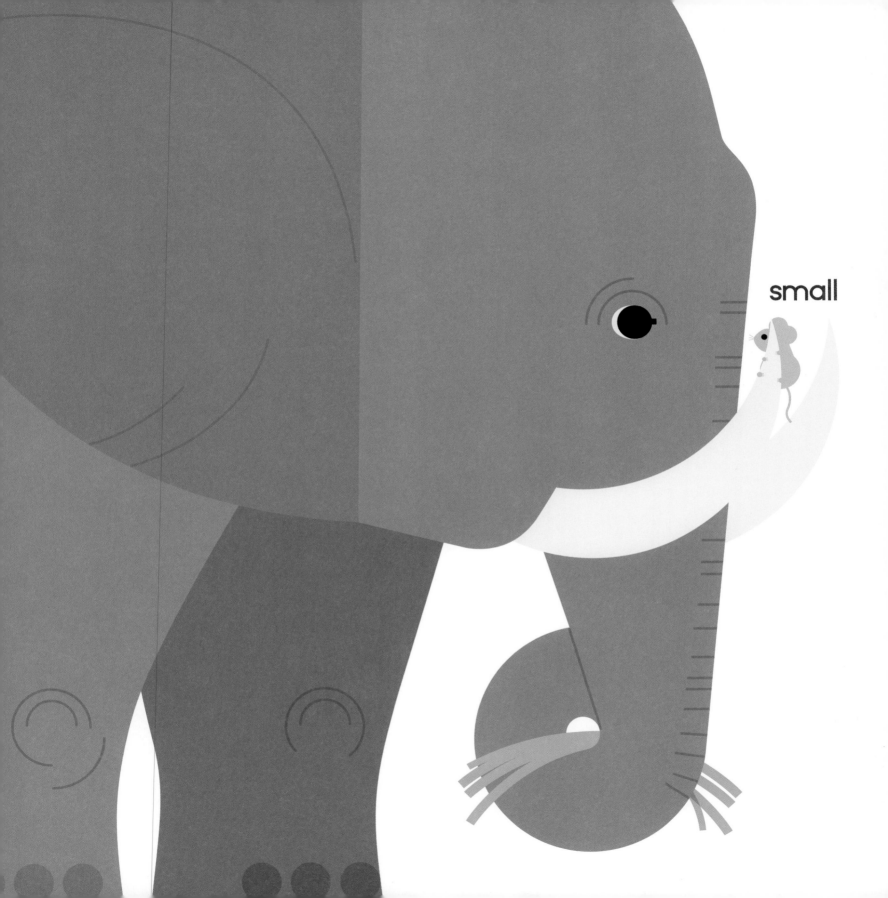

small

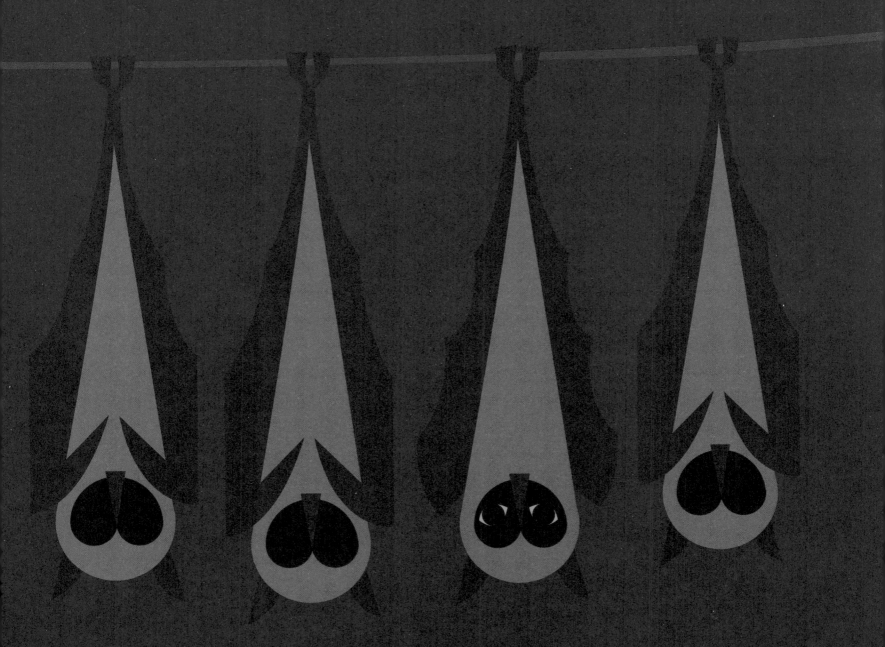

awake

captive

free

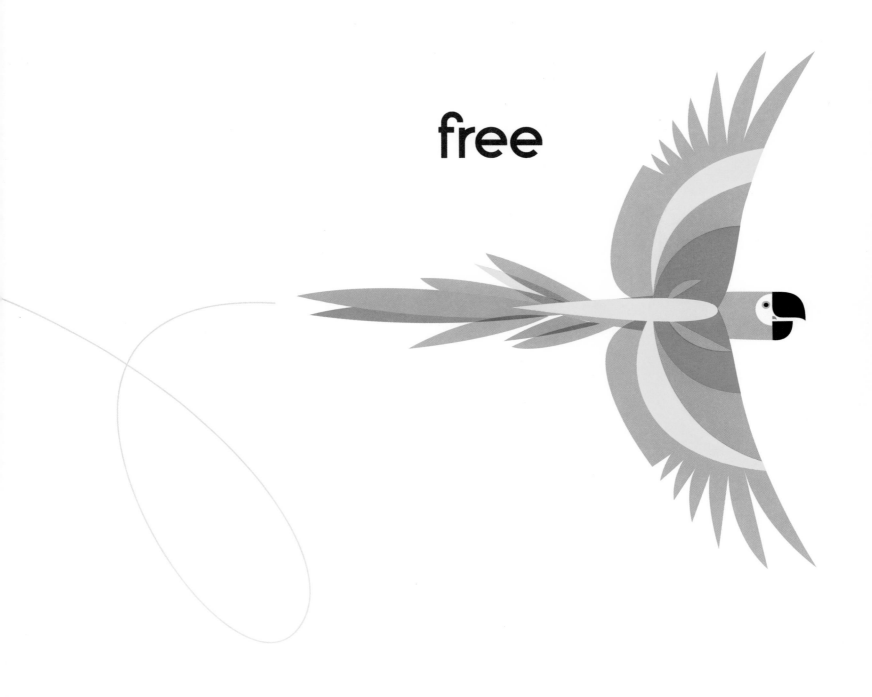

PILLGWENLLY

09-04-18